THE PRINCIPALS OF REPUBLICAN CONSERVATISM

BY PAUL BURKE

ILLUSTRATED BY KENT GAMBLE

Binary PUBLICATIONS

The Principals of Republican Conservatism

Paul Burke ~ Kent Gamble

BINARY PUBLICATIONS LLC

This book is a parody and a work of fiction. Any similarities to people, including likenesses and all the researchers, data aggregators, editors and the information regulator (who happens to be my dog), living or dead is purely fictitious and coincidental.

THIS BOOK IS PUBLISHED IN TWO VERSIONS.
DEMOCRATIC & REPUBLICAN
(why should we limit ourselves to 50% of the buying public?)

Research:
Hua Yu
Rick LeMoyer
LeMoyer Rick
M.Y. Opinion

Data Aggregators:
Buzz Teilowell
Cyd E. Street

Editor:
Petunia Powers

Information Regulator:
Loui Burke

DEDICATION

The authors wish to dedicate this book to Section 107
of the doctrine of Fair Use in the United States Copyright Law
and all the privileges it grants to the creative community.

"We all do better when we work together. Our differences do matter, but our common humanity matters more."
William J. Clinton

"The nine most terrifying words in the English language are, 'I'm from the government and I'm here to help.'"
Ronald Reagan

"Coming together is a beginning.
Keeping together is progress.
Working together is success."
Henry Ford

The Principals of Republican Conservatism

The Principals of Republican Conservatism

The Principals of Republican Conservatism

The Principals of Republican Conservatism

The Principals of Republican Conservatism

The Principals of Republican Conservatism

The Principals of Republican Conservatism

The Principals of Republican Conservatism

The Principals of Republican Conservatism

The Principals of Republican Conservatism

The Principals of Republican Conservatism

The Principals of Republican Conservatism

The Principals of Republican Conservatism

The Principals of Republican Conservatism

The Principals of Republican Conservatism

The Principals of Republican Conservatism

The Principals of Republican Conservatism

ʃ

The Principals of Republican Conservatism

The Principals of Republican Conservatism

The Principals of Republican Conservatism

The Principals of Republican Conservatism

The Principals of Republican Conservatism

The Principals of Republican Conservatism

The Principals of Republican Conservatism

The Principals of Republican Conservatism

The Principals of Republican Conservatism

The Principals of Republican Conservatism

The Principals of Republican Conservatism

The Principals of Republican Conservatism

The Principals of Republican Conservatism

The Principals of Republican Conservatism

The Principals of Republican Conservatism

The Principals of Republican Conservatism

The Principals of Republican Conservatism